MIND-WASHING IN AMERICA

A Conspiracy Against Liberty

... *By* ...

SENATOR JACK B. TENNEY

25c per copy   *6 copies, $1.00*

CHRISTIAN NATIONALIST CRUSADE

P. O. Box 27895   *Los Angeles 27, California*

ISBN: 978-2-925369-48-6
Printed in the USA.

Edward Hunter's revealing book, *"Brain Washing In Red China,"* is overwhelming evidence that the brain changing process graphically pictured in George Orwell's book, "1984," is already in its initial stages. As a matter of fact the "brain-changing" process is proceeding at a rapid rate. The "calculated destruction of men's minds" is the objective behind "thought reform"; mass robot conformity the ultimate goal.

How far has "brain-washing" advanced in the United States?

Is the "E" in UNESCO an essential ingredient in the process?

What is "mental health"?

What is the *Southern California Society for Mental Hygiene?* Why is it supported by the Community Chest? Does it have anything to do with "brain-washing" and "thought-reform" in America?

A yellow brochure tells us that the *Southern California Society for Mental Hygiene* is "a citizens organization dedicated to improving the mental health of the community and its citizens!" Consequently it is a self-appointed group of private individuals that has the impudence to infer mental deficiency to Southern California communities and citizens. To "improve mental health" means that there is room for improvement—and "room for improvement" indicates any given degree from idiocy to utter madness.

The writer would be the last one to contend that complete sanity exists throughout the world—or in Southern California for that matter—but he would certainly challenge the credentials of a "citizens organization" which declares that it is "dedicated to improving the mental health of the community and its citizens" and that it possesses the program and the remedy for improvement.

The headquarters of the Southern California Society for Mental Hygiene is located at 3067 West Seventh Street in Los Angeles. Mrs. Douglas G. Shearer was President in 1951; William B. Miller, 1st Vice-President; Mrs. Frances Corey, 2nd Vice-President; Edward W. Mehren, treasurer, and Mrs. Russell W. Kimble, secretary. The Board of Directors was composed of the following: Lester F. Beck, Margaret E. Bennett, Mrs. Frances Corey, Mrs. Paul Hartmen, Dr. W. Burlin Humphrey, Mrs. Joseph Kaplan, Richard Kilpatrick, Mrs. Russell W. Kimble, Dr. Norman A. Levy, Edward W. Mehren, Mortimer M. Meyer, William B. Miller, Mrs. William Murdock, Dr. Harry H. Nierenberg, Dr. Harriett B. Randall, Dr. James H. Rankin, Mrs. Arthur Raymond, John L. Rowland, Mrs. John Edward Reid, Dr. Philip A. Reynolds, William A. Ring, Mrs. C. Morley Sellery, Mrs. Douglas G. Shearer, Robert Triest, Lulu K. Wolf, Mrs. Arthur S. Wolpe, and Mrs. Ben Zukor. The "staff" consisted of Chauncey A. Alexander, executive director; Beatrice L. Kotas, assistant director; Marilyn J. Page, office secretary; Mae Bucklew, typist clerk, and Kenneth W. Rottger, bookkeeper.

The "Educational Materials Committee" of the Southern California Society for Mental Hygiene issues a pamphlet "revised June, 1952" containing a list of booklets "written by educators, psychiatrists, psychologists and social workers concerned with child development, parent-child relations, social and educational problems as they relate to mental health." Among these "educators, psychiatrists, psychologists and social workers" we find Maxwell S. Stewart; among the publishers of the pamphlets "as they relate to mental health" we discover the Anti-Defamation League of B'Nai B'Rith.

You will find Maxwell S. Stewart's impressive fellow-traveling record digested in the Eighth Report of the California Senate Investigating Committee on Education at pages 66 and 67.

The Anti-Defamation League's concern for your "mental health" is partially covered in *Zion's Fifth Column*.

*　*　*　*

Mrs. Rae Suchman, a crusader for America and Americanism, spends considerable time in versifying her political thinking, thus jabbing the sagging courage of many public officials. Her latest is one of her best and merits preservation in printer's ink:

> *Birds of a feather flock together—*
> *So do pigs and swine—*
> *This goes for the Reds and duped mush-heads—*
> *Who follow the Communist Party line.*

II.

The Southern California Society for Mental Hygiene is affiliated with the County Conference on Community Relations, which maintains headquarters at 3125 West Adams Blvd., in Los Angeles. Among other affiliates of the CCCR are the following: American Jewish Committee, American Jewish Congress, Anti-Defamation League of B'Nai B'Rith, Jewish Community Relations Council, Jewish Labor Committee, Jewish Personnel Relations Bureau, Jewish War Veterans of the U. S. A., International Ladies Garment Workers Union, L. A. Cloak Joint Board, ILGWU, L. A. Sportswear Joint Council, ILGWU, L. A. Dress Joint Board, ILGWU, and the National Conference of Christians and Jews.

That the County Conference on Community Relations divides Americans into segments—"minorities vs. the majority," is self-evident from the foregoing partial list of affiliates. It was "organized to coordinate and unite"; to provide "up-to-the-minute facts, films and literature as well as speakers on community problems, especially where discrimination now exists." It works in "employment," "housing," "education," "law--enforcement," and "youth activities."

The organization supports FEPC legislation, UNESCO and the United Nations. As far as the visible record discloses, its activities may be described as following the Anti-Defamation League line without deviation.

Some selections from CCCR recommended reading: *"Roads to Agreement"* by Stuart Chase; *"International Covenant on Human Rights,"* an AAUN reprint of an address by O. Frederick Nolde, *United Nations World,* October, 1952—three articles for U. N. Week; *McCalls*—September, October, 1952—*"Dangers Ahead in the Public Schools"* by John Bainbridge; *New Outlook*—October, 1952—*"Patriotism for Americans"* by Chet Huntley; and *"Answers to Criticisms on the United Nations and UNESCO"* by Cyrus Barnum.

Among the active members of the County Conference on Community Relations who are also officers of the Southern California Society for Mental Hygiene are Edward W. Mahren, Chauncey Alexander and Mrs. Arthur Wolpe. Milton A. Senn, Joseph Roos, Phil Lerman, Frank Mankiewicz and Irving Hill are ADL members who have been conspicuous in committee activities of the CCCR.

Many of the members of the CCCR are cited in the reports of the California Committee on Un-American Activities or Congressional Committees. The following are a few examples:

David Ziskind: 1948 California Report, pages 35 and 265. International Judicial Association, cited as a Communist front "closely associated with the 'legal arm of the Communist Party,' the International Labor Defense." Ziskind is also cited at pages 795, 801, and 1016, Appendix IX, House Committee on Un-American Activities. David Ziskind is listed as the chairman of CCCR's "legal committee" in CCCR literature. Other members of this committee are: Allan M. Carson, Benjamin Chipkin, Basil Feinberg, Philip Glusker, Mrs. Ruth Goldberg, Max E. Greenberg, Irving Hill, Garland H. Puckett, Nathan L. Schoichet, Herbert W. Simmons, Herman Stern, Abraham Gorenfeld, Alvin P. Jackson, Morris T. Johnson, Abe Levy, David Lippert, Loren Miller, Fred Okrand, Rudy Pacht, Everett M. Porter, Richard Pretherbridge, Anthony Randle, A. L. Wirin, Daniel Marshall and Fred Rosenbaum.

Of the foregoing committee members no less than five have citations in the reports of the California Committee on Un-American Activities.

(See the Index in the 1951 California Report.)

III.

Both Joseph Roos and Milton A. Senn are active Executive Committee members of the Los Angeles County Conference on Community Relations. Mr. Roos is listed as a representative of the Jewish Community Council's Community Relations Committee. Mr. Senn is one of the leading agents of Los Angeles' Anti-Defamation League of B'Nai B'Rith. These two gentlemen, ably assisted of course, keep the organization on the A. D. L. line.

Chauncey Alexander, Executive Director of the Southern California Society for Mental Hygiene and, according to the 1947 Report of the California Committee on Un-American Activities (page 189), an international representative of the Federation of Architects, Engineers, Chemists and Technicians, is a member of CCCR's Education Committee, co-chairmaned by Dr. W. Henry Cooke and Robert Tapp. Other members of this Committee include Sigmund Arywitz of the International Ladies Garment Workers Union, Mrs. Edmond M. Lazard of the American Jewish Committee, Joseph Roos, mentioned above, Fred Schreiber of the American Jewish Committee, Mrs. Fay Rosenblatt of the Metro YWCA, Mrs. Claire Wolpe of the American Jewish Congress, and Max Mont of the Jewish Labor Committee.

"The Education Committee," declares a CCCR report, "became vitally interested in a broad support of public education in a period when organized attacks upon the schools were coming from groups that we considered dangerous to free democratic life. . . The County Conference. . . also entered the public debates, on the 'E in UNESCO' study-guide, at the meetings of the Board of Education. . . and it brought forward in the debate prominent citizens to speak for free democratic education—among them Mr. Paul Hoffman."

Floyd Covington of the Federal Housing Administration is a member of CCCR's Employment Committee. Mr. Covington is included in a list of sponsors for a testimonial dinner for Leo Gallagher (page 8585, Volume 14, House Committee on Un-American Activities). Mr. Gallagher was long connected with Communist fronts and ran for public office in California on the Communist Party ticket. Covington is designated in a CCCR report as "Race Relations Advisor."

The 1952 report of the Unemployment Committee of CCCR reveals that from time to time the Anti-Defamation League carries on surveys to ascertain the extent of "discriminatory" want ads in the Los Angeles metropolitan newspapers. The Committe reports that people continue to advertise for what they want or prefer and this well established principle of American freedom "represents a substantial problem" according to ADL and CCCR thinking. (Of course the Committee doesn't express it this way!) "We, therefore," declares CCCR, "considered it important to take necessary steps to secure a voluntary agreement on the part of newspaper publishers, to refrain from accepting such discriminatory advertising."

The "necessary steps" referred to are not fully described, although it appears that a delegation descended on Floyd Maxwell, Chairman of the Los Angeles Newspaper Publishers Association and flooded him "at his request . . . with a good deal of factual material."

The Committee gives recognition to the "valuable assistance" rendered by Max Greenberg, Harold Roth and David Ziskind "in doing the necessary legal research" for the Committee's projects.

* * * *

Incidentally, Dr. A. C. Kinsey, sex authority, was to speak on "Sexual Adjustment in the Human Female" at the Greek Theatre August 25th, 1953.

His lecture was publicized as being "under the auspices of the Southern California Society for Mental Hygiene."

What do you make of this, Watson?

IV.

The present headquarters of the Southern California Society for Mental Hygiene is a small store-front space about twenty by twenty-five feet (more or less) on West Seventh Street, a few doors east of Vermont on the north side of the street. The walls are lined with book-shelves stocked with pamphlets and booklets. Current promotion is Dr. Kinsey and his "sex" studies.

The Society appears to place considerable emphasis on sex in its pursuit of "mental hygiene." Dr. Margaret Read, author of *"Male and Female, Coming of Age in Samoa,"* was a featured speaker under Society auspices at the Los Angeles High School Auditorium on Friday, April 17, 1953. On July 1 and 2, 1953, the Society presented a French film "with English titles" entitled *"Passion For Life"*—advertised by the Society as "the simplest and most convincing exposition of progressive philosophies and teaching methods yet presented to the American public." On July 22 and 23 "First Lessons" and "Shyness" were previewed under Society auspices at the Institute of Aeronautical Sciences Auditorium. The first film is a production of the National Mental Health Film Board— the sixth of a series. "Shyness" is alleged to have been released by the Canadian Mental Health Film Board.

Susan D. Adams, as heretofore pointed out, is not only an active member of the Southern California Society for Mental Hygiene but also active in the Los Angeles County Conference on

Community Relations. Chauncey Alexander, Executive Director of the Southern California Society for Mental Hygiene, is another individual who is active in the LACCCR. In addition to having been an International Representative of the Communist dominated Federation of Architects, Engineers, Chemists and Technicians (FAECT), he was a member of Communist controlled State, County and Municipal Workers (SCMWA), according to the *Labor Herald* for December 24, 1943.

In April of 1953 the Society, through its President Mrs. William D. Murdock, announced "a momentous decision, vital to the future of the mental health field in Southern California." This "momentous decision," declared Mrs. Murdock, was a determination to participate in the first National Mental Health Fund Drive, which was scheduled for May of 1953. "Campaign participation," averred the President, "required withdrawal from the L. A. Community Chest to expand organization of the mental health movement in Southern California.

Judge Thurmond Clarke was induced to act as "Campaign Chairman." Headquarters were established at 116 South La Brea Ave. in Los Angeles and the Southern California Health Fund drive was on. "Give to Fight Mental Illness" and "Ring the Bell for Mental Health" were slogans for the drive—and the goal was $320,000! It was announced that "about" 20% of the money raised would go toward the support of the National Association for Mental Health and the remainder "toward support of mental health programs in local communities of Southern California."

On Thursday, May 7, 1953, Isaac Pacht became Los Angeles County chairman of the $320,000 campaign drive, according to an article on Page A-6 of the Los Angeles Herald Express of that date.

As an interesting and perhaps significant sidelight, the Southern California Society for Mental Hygiene recommended that the Los Angeles City Council adopt legislation "to protect people from quack psychologists"—asserting that Los Angeles is "a breeding ground for charlatans posing as psychologists."

V.

The Los Angeles County Conference on Community Relations, pursuant to a resolution submitted by Sigmund Arywitz of the International Ladies Garment Workers Union, established a Committee on Evaluation and Organization in 1952. Susan Adams of the American Federation of Labor chairmans this committee. Among its members we find Sigmund Arywitz, Mrs. Adele Denton of B'Nai B'Rith Women, Zane Meckler of the Jewish Community Relations Committee, Max Mont of the Jewish Labor Committee and Phillip Lerman of the Anti-Defamation League.

The purpose of this particular committee is a "continuous year-round review of the CCCR's organizational processes and procedures" in order that regular recommendations for "improvement" may be made. The committee has been working on "broader agency participation on LACCCR committees" and "changes in the Conference rules of procedure and administrative practices." Conscious of the importance of titles in the field of propaganda the committee recommended changing the name of the Police Relations Committee to Committee on Law Enforcement, thus camouflaging race agitation in the criminal field under the color of law and order. Among other proposals was a new standing Committee on Health and Medicine—immediately adopted of course—thus extending racial agitation to the hospital bed.

The new Committee on Health and Medicine, although barely organized, was able to stir up muddy waters without delay, thanks to the untiring efforts of Dale Gardner of the County Committee on Human Relations and Milton Senn of the Anti-Defamation League. Both of these gentlemen came forward with "evidence of discrimination in Medical schools, in health plans, and in hospitals against both minority group patients and doctors"—so that Margaret Olson of the Citizens Housing Council and Max Mont of the Jewish Labor Committee were able to whip up a report in no time at all for the President's Commission on the Health Needs of the Nation. The Anti-Defamation League, Jewish Labor Committee and the International Ladies Garment Workers Union, among others, sponsored the report—indicating, of course, the impartial and factual nature of the document. No other group had found anything to complain about as "the CCCR report was apparently the only one of its nature presented before the Commission on the west coast."

The Committee on Health and Medicine adopted the full program of the A. D. L. for race agitation. It was undertaken to coordinate programs for ferreting out "discrimination in health services"; publicizing the "success of democratic health practices" and snooping into the training and practice of doctors "and other health personnel" whether public or private.

Among those serving on the Committee were Max Mont of the Jewish Labor Committee, Dr. Edward Shapiro, Chairman, Division of Medicine, General Hospital; Dr. Max Igloe, Director, International Ladies Garment Workers Union Health Center; Louis Ziskind, President, American Association Social Workers; Dr. Max Bay, County Committee on Human Relations; Chauncey Alexander, Southern California Society for Mental Hygiene, and Abe Friedman of the Workmens Circle.

It should be apparent that the County Conference on Community Relations is strictly a front for the Anti-Defamation League of B'Nai B'Rith and that it serves the purposes of organized Jewry.

VI.

Having surveyed the organizational composition of the Los Angeles County Conference on Community Relations and the apparent interlocking control of the Southern California Society for Mental Hygiene it would appear profitable to search for organized Jewry's influence in the latter group.

It is not difficult to find.

As has been noted both organizations, under one pretext or another, use the shield of their purported purposes for racial agitation. In view of Anti-Defamation League's reiterated assertions that "anti-Semitism" is a "mental disorder" it becomes doubly important to consider its role in such an organization as the Southern California Society for Mental Hygiene.

Intermingled among recommended pamphlets on "Mental Health"—which include pearls of wisdom by such writers as Maxwell S. Stewart and Dr. William Heard Kilpatrick—we find the propaganda of the Anti-Defamation League of B'Nai B'Rith. The very fact that this appears to be the only secret society contributing such material is at once arresting and somewhat alarming. Neither the "Fraternal Order of Eagles" nor the "Benevolent and Protective Order of Elks" seem to have contributed a pamphlet—and there is not a single recommendation for anything whatever produced by the "Knights of Columbus." But the ADL line is unmistakably represented.

Pamphlet No. 800 is the "ABC's of Scapegoating"—a favorite ADL propaganda line that alibis Bonds for Israel, dual citizenship and the invasion of Palestine. This opus is by Gordon W. Allport, sells for 30 cents and contains 56 pages. It is alleged by SCSMH to be "a comprehensive exposition of the basic mechanisms and conditions of prejudice and scapegoating in America today." If you are unaware of "scapegoating in America" it is to be assumed that your "mental health" is pretty badly impaired. This ADL pamphlet is undoubtedly the "hygiene" you need or—in lieu thereof institutional correction may be necessary.

Pamphlet No. 802, produced by the Anti-Defamation League of B'Nai B'Rith and highly recommended by the SCSMH is provocatively titled "How Do You Talk About People?" by Irving J. Lee. It sells for two-bits and contains 38 pages. Furthermore it is labeled "A Freedom Pamphlet." Do you talk about people out of the corner of your mouth? Do you have your tongue in your cheek? These, and other unique manners of discussing people are not *per se* signs of mental derangement. Do you discuss people in English, French or pig-latin? Do you use broad or short "a"-s? If you merely discuss your neighbors in any of the usual ways you may escape commitment to Camarillo. The question is whether or not you occasionally recognize some racial quality and call a spade a spade. You may still retain your sanity by referring to an Irishman as a "Mick" and you may sometimes call an Italian a "wop"—but you are in need of "mental hygiene" if you call a Jew a Jew or criticize organized Jewry. Irving J. Lee is advertised by SCSMH as "an expert in semantics." In Pamphlet No. 802 he "analyses the errors in thinking about other people."

While we haven't had an opportunity to read this work we do not hesitate to place it in that section of our library classified as "brain-washing in the United States"—along with two other ADL pamphlets numbered 805 and 806.

VII.

The San Francisco Mental Health Society appears to be Northern California's replica of the Southern California Society for Mental Hygiene. It is also a recipient of Community Chest funds. Its headquarters are located at 998 Eddy Street in San Francisco. Its President is William A. Bellamy, M. D.

The political disposition of this outfit is strongly indicated by a letter addressed to "all committee members" under date of April 21, 1953., and signed by Dr. Bellamy. Writes the President: "The San Francisco Mental Health Society most respectfully urges your support of AB 900, as amended. The society believes that the welfare of all citizens of California can best be served by facing this issue squarely and forthrightly. . . This proposed legislation, if passed, will go a long way to relieve tensions, overcome unfortunate prejudices, and certainly will have far-reaching benefits. Furthermore, it will encourage employers to employ qualified and acceptable persons regardless of race, religion, color or national origin. The mental health of all concerned will be greatly benefited. We trust that you will give vigorous support to AB 900 and do your part to bring California into line with the nine other states who have similar legislation. . . "

Many members of the Legislature, including the Senator from Los Angeles County, believe that FEPC legislation (AB 900) is Communist inspired. Assembly Bill 900 died in the Assembly in spite of the efforts of the San Francisco Mental Health Society—and the many pressure groups advocating its passage.

Among the members of the Board of Directors of the San Francisco Mental Health Society may be mentioned Philip Adams, a member of the Executive Committee of the American Civil Liberties Union (Daily People's World, October 28, 1940, and letterhead ACLU November 1, 1940).

Among others Dr. Herbert C. Clish, Rabbi Alvin I. Fine, Daniel E. Koshland, Rev. Harry C. Meserve, Dr. Norman Reider, George V. Sheviakov, Rev. Howard Thurman, Rabbi Saul E. White and Dr. Ernst Wolff are members of the SFMHS Advisory Council.

The *Daily People's World* for August 2, 1950, announced that Dr. Herbert C. Clish was one of those who would "defend the San Francisco Schools" against "Hearstian smearing,"—undoubtedly referring to the Hearst papers campaign against Communism in the Public Schools.

In August of 1952 Rabbi Alvin I. Fine was sponsor for the Federation For Repeal of the Levering Act. (The Levering Act was an anti-Communist law providing for loyalty oaths. It was overwhelmingly approved by the people of California when they adopted a Constitutional Amendment embodying the principles of the Levering Act.)

The name of Dan E. Koshland appears at pages 89 and 93 of the 1947 Report of the California Committee on Un-American Activities as a sponsor, in 1946 and 1947, of the California Labor School, listed by the Committee as a Communist front organization.

The Rev. Harry C. Meserve is listed as a sponsor of the Federation For Repeal of the Levering Act in a pamphlet distributed in August, 1952. He is also listed (February, 1953) as a sponsor of the "Farm Labor Newsletter" and a member of the San Francisco Inter-Faith Committee for Peace. (*Daily People's World*, March 17, 1953).

The foregoing citations are not to be considered evidence that those named are Communists or even pro-Communist or Communist sympathizers. Many of them may consider themselves anti-Communist in this day when it is not considered fashionable to be for "good old Joe" and all he stood for. All of them may be good-intentioned dupes;—plain old "do-gooders" with the best intentions in the world;—innocents who swallow any line labeled "tolerance," brotherhood or ADL. The citations, regardless of what they tend to prove, do, however, offer a fair sample of the mental processes of the individuals who have appointed themselves guardians of the mental health of San Francisco.

VIII.

Andre Emery, columnist and writer, is the Executive Director of the San Francisco Mental Health Society. The *Daily People's World*, West Coast issue of New York's Communist sheet, the *Daily Worker*, for September 15, 1949, informed its readers that Andre Emery was to report on the Mexican Peace Conference—a Communist conclave for Soviet objectives. In

1950 Mr. Emery was a Spring Term Instructor at the California Labor School in San Francisco—cited as a Communist front organization.

Both Dr. Norman Reider and the Rev. Howard Thurman, members of the Advisory Council of the SFMHS were sponsors of the Federation For Repeal of the Levering Act.

Rabbi Saul White of Temple Beth Sholum is another member of the Advisory Council of SFMHS. In January, 1940, he was a sponsor of the Conference for Democratic Action held in Fresno. The *Daily People's World* for April 16, 1940, announced that Rabbi White was to be a speaker at the International Labor Defense Town Talk Series on April 21 at 83 McAllister Street in San Francisco. An Attorney General of the United States labeled the International Labor Defense "the legal arm of the Communist Party." The *Daily People's World* for August 9, 1941, announced that Rabbi White asserted that Communist Darcy should be released on bail pending appeal. The same paper (December 4, 1943) listed Rabbi White as a sponsor of American Youth for Democracy, reported by Legislative Committees as the successor organization to the Young Communist League. The *Daily People's World* (March 17, 1953) lists Rabbi White as a member of San Francisco's Inter-Faith Committee for Peace.

Dr. Ernst Wolff, member of the Advisory Council of SFMHS has been a speaker at the Tom Mooney School in San Francisco (*Daily People's World,* January 22, 1943); member of a group organized to defeat the Dilworth Bill outlawing the Communist Party in California (*Daily People's World,* November 26, 1943); signer of a telegram with Leona Wolff addressed to Senator Jack B. Tenney opposing anti-Communist legislation before the 1951 Session of the Legislature (April 19, 1951), and a signer of plea for amnesty for the U. S. Communist leaders convicted under the Smith Act addressed to President Truman (*Daily People's World,* December 9, 1952).

George V. Sheviakov (Sheviakoff) was a teacher at the California Labor School, according to the *Labor Herald,* December 29, 1944. He was then connected with the University of California Child Guidance Center. (See *Daily People's World* for January 2, 1945, page 5, columns 4 and 5). The same paper for January 6, 1945, reports that Sheviakov was connected with the Institute of Child Welfare. DPW for March 7, 1945, announced that Sheviakov was Research Assistant at the Institute of Child Welfare at the University of California and that he was a "visiting lecturer" of a course "Everyday Problems of Pre-School Child" at the Oakland Branch of the California Labor School.

In August, 1952, Sheviakov participated in a panel under the auspices of Station KRON-TV and the San Francisco Mental Health Society entitled "What's On Your Mind?"

Since April, 1953, Mr. Sheviakov has been lecturing at the University of California at Los Angeles. In addition he is a "consultant to Elementary School Principles in Pasadena" at $45.00 per consultation of the tax-payers' money.

IX

The Housing Committee of the County Conference on Community Relations is heavily staffed with representatives of organized Jewry. Among its members in 1952 we find Sigmund Arywitz of the International Ladies Garment Workers Union, Nat Feder of the Welfare Council, Abe Levy, Frank Mankiewicz of the Anti-Defamation League of B'Nai B'Rith, Max Mont of the Jewish Labor Committee, Mrs. Fay Rosenblatt of the League of Women Voters, Frederick Schreiber of the American Jewish Committee and Al Weinberg of the Jewish War Veterans. The Committee found itself grateful to the American Jewish Committee for "assigning" Louis Mazer to serve the group "as its convener."

This Committee of CCCR is interested in "preserving" public housing. Consequently Floyd Covington, "Race Relations Advisor" of the Federal Housing Administration, is a member of the Committee; a fact that indicates the open-mindedness of the group! In its 1952 report the Committee recognized "the tremendous task of reducing residential antagonism" to public housing but expressed the hope that it will "deal seriously with methods of meeting this issue."

The Joint Staff of CCCR became alarmed in 1952 when a citizens' group undertook to study text-books for Communist and subversive propaganda. This sort of thing is almost as objectionable to these Jews as "McCarthyism" and is interpreted by CCCR as "an attack on the public schools" by "groups"

THE MOST DANGEROUS BOOK IN THE WORLD
WHAT IS IT?

1. Henry Ford, Sr., published a review of this book, and mysterious forces threatened to kidnap his grandchildren.

2. Mrs. Henry Ford, Sr., begged her husband to stop publishing this book because of thousands of anonymous threats she received through the mail and over the telephone from people who threatened to murder her illustrious husband.

3. One man in Canada, an outstanding patriot, served five years in prison because he published the facts contained in this book.

4. In 1942 numerous individuals were indicted, and but for a miracle would have been framed up and sentenced to the Federal Penitentiary because they circulated the information contained in this book.

5. The Christian Nationalist Crusade, directed by Gerald L. K. Smith is the only organization in America now publishing and circulating this deadly document.

6. Behind the 'iron curtain' all the publishers and journalists who published this book have been shot or sentenced to lifetime enslavement.

RARE CHANCE TO OBTAIN <u>FREE</u> COPY

One of the three most important members of the United States Senate recently said concerning **The Cross and the Flag**:

"it is the most correct periodical in America because it deals fearlessly and intelligently with the real issues of this terrific moment."

The Cross and the Flag is noted for its courage to deal with subjects which strike fear and terror in the hearts of most editors and publishers. Every member of the United States Senate and every member of the House of Representatives receives every issue of this magazine. Truth contained in The Cross and the Flag finds its way into the thinking and speeches of many members of Congress. No American citizen who wants to know the full score can afford to be without this fearless crusading periodical.

If you subscribe at $2.00 per year immediately, you may have a copy of the above-mentioned book FREE.

The Title of the Book Is:
THE PROTOCOLS of the LEARNED ELDERS of ZION

This is the mysterious bound volume of the secret minutes of the International Jewish Council which met in 1905 and planned to capture control of the world. Over half of what they committed themselves to do has already been accomplished. It is the most amazing document ever to be put in print.

If you already have a copy you owe it to your best friend to get a copy for him, and this is your chance to get it free. We know of no other place in America where you can obtain it. Bookstores are afraid to sell it. Printers are afraid to publish it. Every intelligent American citizen should know why certain forces fear the terrific truth contained in this dynamic document.

THE CROSS AND THE FLAG
Post Office Box 27895
Los Angeles 27, California

Please enter my subscription to The Cross and the Flag at $2.00 per year, which I enclose herewith. It is understood that I am to receive a free copy of the most dangerous book in the world: "The Protocols of the Learned Elders of Zion."

NAME ....

ADDRESS ....

CITY .... ZONE .... STATE........................

CCCR considers "dangerous to free democratic life." The Joint staff is willing to concede "the right of citizens to study text-books" but is very much concerned about "the methods used" by the citizens. Undoubtedly some citizens study text-books standing up while others prefer a sitting or reclining method. A few unusual citizens may have a method of studying text-books while standing on their heads—a rather curious way of study-ing text-books to be sure but hardly any business of the Joint Staff of CCCR. What the Joint Staff actually means is that it is interested in the conclusions of citizens' groups screening text-books. In order to meet and combat conclusions contrary to ADL directives CCCR's Joint Staff set up an Ad Hoc Com-mittee on Text-Books.

The Conference runs into major obstacles on occasion. Its totalitarian process of wagging the democratic dog by its demo-cratic tail doesn't always work and there are frustrating mo-ments when the American majority refuse to have ADL dogma crammed down its collective throat. The overwhelming Los Angeles vote against public housing was one such occasion. But the Anti-Defamation League of B'Nai B'Rith is not easily discouraged. A proposed ordinance designed to create a Com-mission on Human Relations drafted by CCCR's Legal Com-mittee was finally abandoned as "politically unattainable"— but the Committee persevered, exploring suggestions to by-pass the people's duly elected legislative body—the City Council— and achieve "the same objective" by executive action of the Mayor.

It would appear that the alien method of "back-stair" di-plomacy is being extended by the Anti-Defamation League to its fronts and stooges.

Joseph Roos of the Jewish Community Council is Chairman of the Radio and Television Committee of the County Confer-ence on Community Relations. He was probably responsible for a weekly black-out on Television Channel KTTV in 1952 when "The World in Your Hands" was presented. In any event, Roos thanks Station KTTV "for making time available."

Dr. Ella Kube heads up CCCR's Research Committee. Among the members we find Dr. Ralph Beals of U. C. L. A., Bernard Coleman, Louis Mazer and Seymour Soroky, all of the AJC.

It appears that Dr. Ella Kube did not accomplish too much in 1952. "The work of the Research Committee," she declared, "has been handicapped by the fact that participation by member agencies has been negligible. The American Jewish Committee which has had two representatives at all meetings has been a most valuable exception."

Evelyn Mathews is the Chairman of CCCR's Youth Activities Committee. Chauncey Alexander of the Southern California Society for Mental Hygiene, Phil Lerman of the Anti-Defamation League, Mrs. Sylvia Leventhal of B'Nai B'Rith Women, and Herbert Liebowitz are some of the members of this group.

"One of the first steps in serving the youth agencies and organizations," says the Committee's 1952 report, "would be the compilation of a resource directory. Judy Cozzens (Welfare Council), Louis Mazer (American Jewish Committee) assisted by the County Conference staff, has prepared such a directory . . . "

Mrs. Jack Hardy co-chairs CCCR's Finance Committee. "The Finance Committee," reports Mrs. Hardy in 1952, "faced the problem at the start of this year of replacing the financial grant assistance given by the American Missionary Association and the Council for Social Action, both being divisions of the General Council of Congregational Christian Churches. It was through such assistance that the LACCCR was able to launch its staffed program back in 1948. We are grateful to the Congregational Christian Churches for this support and especially for their willingness to extend the support beyond the customary three year period."

Mrs. Hardy reports that a Thanksgiving luncheon was held November 15, 1951, "at which contributions and pledges amounting to $5,295.00 were received." The affair was held under the sponsorship of "Attorney Jack W. Hardy, Judge Isaac Pacht, Mr. George A. Beavers, Jr., Mrs. Sumner Spaulding, and County Supervisor John Anson Ford. Our hearty thanks," adds Mrs. Hardy, "to Mr. Murray Lewis, Director, Jewish Personnel Relations Bureau, who did a magnificent job in planning and managing the affair."

CCCR's budget for 1952-1953 was $20,250.00.

The Los Angeles County Committee on Human Relations appears to be a piece in the jig-saw puzzle presented by the Southern California Society for Mental Hygiene, the San Francisco Mental Health Society, the Los Angeles County Conference on Community Relations and the Anti-Defamation League of B'Nai B'Rith. In 1952 Miss Nita Blackwell was Chairman of the Los Angeles Committee on Human Relations and it appears that Los Angeles tax-payers were picking up the Committee's checks through the Los Angeles County Board of Supervisors. Joseph Roos was one of three vice-chairmen and T. Dale Gardner was "Community Consultant"—thus assuring complete coordination through the other organizations mentioned above.

Miss Nita Blackwell used "County of Los Angeles" stationery when she addressed the members. On January 3, 1952, she notified the membership that an "important meeting of our general committee" was to be held "in the Board of Supervisors Room of the Hall of Records at 2 P. M. on January 7." The headquarters of the Committee was located at 205 South Broadway and the tax-payers of Los Angeles County paid the phone bill,—MUtual 9211, Extension 3171.

Miss Nita Blackwell is reported to have been the Secretary of the National Association for the Advancement of Colored People (NAACP) and actively connected with the American Jewish Congress. (See Reports of the California Legislative Committee on Un-American Activities).

T. Dale Gardner was registered as a Socialist although he is presently registered as a Democrat.

The purpose of the Los Angeles County Committee on Human Relations—no matter how sugar-coated the phraseology—is inter-racial agitation and propaganda. It not only stands for public housing in a big way—but for inter-racial housing.

One of the interesting projects of the Los Angeles County Committee on Human Relations was the compilation and distribution of what might be called the "Anti-Defamation League's blacklist;"—prepared, according to Miss Blackwell, "from information contained in our files and in a County library book entitled "A Measure of Freedom," by Arnold Forster." (Miss Blackwell did not tell the Board of Supervisors that Arnold Forster was and is general counsel for the Anti-Defamation League of B'Nai B'Rith). Miss Blackwell attempted to explain to the late Supervisor Darby: "The information had been requested by numerous clergymen who had been besieged with anonymous mailings of literature designed to incite hatred of minority groups. In an effort to help churches to identify the sources of such literature, this bulletin was prepared and was distributed by the Lutheran Welfare Council of Los Angeles and the Church Federation of Los Angeles."

And—the job appears to have been financed by good old John Q. Public.

XII.

The Anti-Defamation League's "blacklist" prepared from Arnold Forster's racial-agitation book, *"A Measure of Freedom,"* by the Los Angeles County Committee on Human Relations in December, 1951, is obviously a political devise for silencing critics; critics of Socialism, Communism, New Dealism, and particularly, critics of the Anti-Defamation League.

Among those listed as having "a record of inciting hatred of racial and/or religious minority groups" are the National Council on American Education (devoted to combating Communism in the schools), National Economic Council (fighting for a return to the principles of the United States Constitution), Constitutional Educational League, (anti-Communist, anti-New-Deal, pro-America and pro-Constitutional organization), Christian Nationalist Crusade, (anti-Communist, anti-New Deal, anti-internationalist and anti-dual citizenship group), California Anti-Communist League, Cinema Educational Guild, Keep America Committee, and others.

The political bias and underlying purpose of the Los Angeles County Committee on Human Relations is clearly revealed by its comments on the groups listed. The Anglo-Saxon Christian Congregation, headed by Dr. Wesley Swift, is said to be "anti-United Nations, the U. N. Flag, the National administration, bi-partisan foreign policy, the Roosevelt family," etc. To all of which, I am quite confident, George Washington, Abraham Lincoln and Dr. Swift would all breathe a fervent "Amen."

The Cinema Educational Guild, said to be a conception of

. . . Gerald L. K. Smith, is alleged to be an organization "to expose Communism in Hollywood"—apparently a world shaking indictment in Mr. Forster's book and the minds of the members of LACHR.

Among the horrible activities of the individuals included in the LACHR's "blacklist" are the following:

"Dr. Wesley Swift has attempted to start local groups in Long Beach and El Monte. He has a regular group in Antelope Valley. He has succeeded in obtaining speaking engagements before service clubs in East Hollywood and Laguna Beach."

It is quite plain from these revealing facts (undenied on the part of the culprit, mind you!) that Dr. Swift should be boiled in oil and drawn and quartered. In the well ordered world being prepared for us by LACHR and ADL these activities—particularly that part about speaking before service clubs—will be capital offenses. (Only it will also be a crime to belong to a service club.)

Upton Close and Yusif El Bandak have actually appeared at Los Angeles churches.

Major Robert H. Williams has spoken before service clubs in this County!

The utter lack of honesty and decency on the part of LACHR is obvious in this bit of attempted libel. "Major" is in quotations inducing the reader to infer that the army rank is spurious or, at least, doubtful. "(He) has had his reserve commission taken away from him 'for the good of the service' " is a paradoxical addition in no way intended to build up the Major's reputation in the neighborhood. All officers are ultimately discharged "for the good of the service"—their commissions are not "taken away" from them. It is an honorable discharge, a fact known to all who served their country in uniform—and to most informed people who stayed home, and certainly is well known to the LACHR. The ADL slip is showing rather grotesquely below the LACHR's shoddy apron in this instance.

Gerald L. K. Smith is accused of distributing literature to Protestant Churches in 1950! Such open exercise of American freedom would not be tolerated one second in the Soviet Union! —and, apparently LACHR would like to put a stop to it in Los Angeles. In any event, it just goes to prove what kind of a man this Gerald L. K. Smith is—flying in the face of the ADL and the LACHR! In his exercise of Constitutional guarantees this fellow Smith had the audacity to deliver a "packet of more than 25 items" to Pasadena clergymen during April, 1951! And what is immeasurably worse and a thousand times more reprehensible—although LACHR is silent on this point— the Pasadena clergymen appear to have been happy to have received the packets.

XIII.

In 1952 the Los Angeles Citizens' Committee on Education set up a subcommittee to investigate alleged un-American influences in the public schools. The chief target of investigation was the school textbook. The Sub-Committee spent considerable time and study in working out a thoroughly American criteria for its investigations and ultimately adopted a series of test questions on text-book content for its text-book reviewer's guide in evaluating the Americanism of a given work. Among these test questions were the following:

"Does it (the textbook) point out that the use of taxation can destroy the right of private ownership?

"Does it tell of the progress made toward the attainment of better economic and social conditions without government controls (rising wages, improved living and working conditions, retirement funds, group medical services, educational opportunities, etc.)?

"In presenting both sides of the problem of political and social issues does it identify the subject under discussion or the proposed solution as being a principle of COLLECTIVIST GOVERNMENT, of being a principle of our form of government—INDIVIDUALISM or CAPITALISM?

"If this material discusses government ownership or control of production and services, does it show why this destroys freedom of the lives of those people?

"If it discusses Social Justice, does it make a distinction between Social Justice and Socialism disguised as Social Justice?

"Does this material bring out that ratification of the International Declaration of Human Rights would nullify many of the provisions of the Bill of Rights of the United States of

America and our Constitution?" (See the Constitution of the United States, Article VI, Section 2).

The County Conference on Community Relations, dominated by organized Jewry, went into immediate action against the Los Angeles Citizens Committee on Education and its sub-Committee. An Ad Hoc Committee on Text-Books was appointed. A "statement" on the Citizens' Sub-Committee Investigating Alleged Un-American Influences in the Schools was prepared and Dr. Hugh M. Tiner was induced to present it to the Los Angeles Board of Education December 22, 1952. Said Dr. Tiner, in part:

"Now let me turn to developments which jeopardize the excellent standards which exist in our schools. In times of tension and crisis, such as we live in, it is understandable that some groups might question the goals of public education . . . One such group is the Committee to Investigate Alleged Un-American Influences in our Schools . . . This Committee has adopted as its yardstick an "Outline for Review of Educational Materials' . . . After careful study of this questionnaire, we have found it to be a thoroughly biased, unscientific and unfair yardstick . . . Our statement evaluates this questionnaire in detail, pointing to its loaded character, and concluding that no textbook could be as biased or as unscientific in principle as the questionnaire of this Committee."

After which Dr. Tiner presented the prepared "Statement."

On December 31, 1952, Welty Lefever issued a call for a meeting of CCCR's Ad Hoc Committee on Textbooks for January 7, 1953, in the Board Room of the Jewish Community Council, 590 North Vermont (second floor).

And thus America pays the penalty for its policy of unrestricted immigration. Unable to assimilate American principles, organized Jewry seeks their destruction through Jewish dominated front organizations meeting in Jewish Board rooms.

Thomas Jefferson, in his *Notes on Virginia*, wrote (1782):

"The present desire of America is to produce rapid population by as great importation of foreigners as possible. But is this founded in good policy? . . . Every species of government has its specific principles. Ours perhaps are more peculiar than those of any other in the universe. It is a composition of the freest principles of the English Constitution, with others derived from natural right and natural reason . . . emigrants . . . will bring with them the principles of the governments they leave, imbibed in their early youth; or, if able to throw them off, it will be in exchange for an unbounded licentiousness, passing, as is usual, from one extreme to another. It would be a miracle were they to stop precisely at the point of temperate liberty. These principles, with their language, they will transmit to their children. In proportion to their numbers, they will share with us the legislation. They will infuse into it their spirit, warp and bias its directions, and render it a heterogeneous, incoherent, distracted mass.''

No American, in 1953, will say that Jefferson was wrong in 1782.

XIV.

After addressing the Los Angeles Board of Education, December 22, 1952, Dr. Hugh M. Tiner presented the members with a "Statement" prepared by the Ad Hoc Committee on Text-Books of the County Conference on Community Relations. The statement was endorsed by the American Veterans Committee, American Federation of Teachers, American Jewish Committee, B'Nai B'Rith Women, International Ladies Garment Workers' Union, Jewish Community Relations Committee, Jewish Labor Committee, Knisseth Israel Jr. Sisterhood, Southern California Conference of B'Nai B'Rith Women, Southern California B'Nai B'Rith Council and others.

Among individuals endorsing the statement we find the following: Chauncey Alexander, Sigmund Arywitz, Ralph G. Beals, George Beavers, Leonard I. Beerman, Mrs. H. A. Blumenthal, Rabbi Jehudah M. Cohen, Judy Cozzens, Joseph T. De Silva, Nat Feder, Leon Furgatch, T. Dale Gardner, Helen R. Gottlober, Mrs. Ruth C. Greenberg, Mrs. Jack Hardy, Sam Hartog, Mrs. Edward M. Lazard, Samuel H. Legar, Mrs. Sandra G. Levy, Mrs. Joseph Lowitz, Albert T. Lunceford, George B. Mangold, Mrs. Holly Mankiewicz, Edward W. Mehren, Max Mont, Rudolph Pacht, Mrs. Pearl G. Rothenberg, Nathan L. Schoichet, Dr. Alfred Schuman, Mrs. Milton Seegal, Mrs. Jack J. Spitzer, Isidor Stenzor, Mrs. George B. Taussig, Mrs. J. E. Wolfe and Isidor Elias.

The statement purports to criticize the Sub-Committee's criteria for studying alleged un-Americanism in school textbooks. The alien viewpoint of the endorsers of the statement is clearly indicated by the left-wing nature of the criticism of the Sub-Committee's excellent questionnaire. Following are a few examples:

"Does it (the textbooks) point out that the use of taxation can destroy the right of private ownership? *Comment* (statement to Board): This is evidently a loaded question because it does not contemplate the full discussion of all sides of the taxation question; nor the need for appropriate taxation to operate our government and to assure the defense of the United States of America.

"If it (the textbook) discussed Social Justice, does it make a distinction between Social Justice and Socialism disguised as Social Justice?" *Comment* (statement to Board): This is an attempt to smear as Socialistic attempts to achieve social welfare through government action.

At a further point the "statement" declares: "A matter of serious moment is that nowhere in the questionnaire devoted to the problems of government, economics and society are the words 'democracy' or 'democratic' to be found."

All of which, obviously, indicates the alien-minded attitude of those who drafted and endorsed the statement. Most Americans know that the power to tax is the power to destroy; that there is a big difference between "social justice" and socialism; that "social welfare" through governmental action is socialism, and that the words "democracy" and "democratic" are no where to be found in the Constitution of the United States or the Bill of Rights. When we pledge allegiance, we pledge ourselves to the flag . . . and to the *Republic* for which it stands.

Lenin often spoke and wrote about "democracy"—although the founders of our nation and the authors of the Constitution rejected it as a form of government that gravitated to totalitarianism and despotism—as in Lenin's Soviet Union. Said Lenin: "Just as Socialism cannot be victorious unless it introduces complete democracy, so the proletariat will be unable to prepare for victory over the bourgeoisie unless it wages a many-sided consistent and revolutionary struggle for democracy."

Looking over the enslaved masses of Russia, Lenin wrote: "Comparison of social conditions in the Soviet Union, where the toilers enjoy full power, with the limited democracy of capitalist countries explains why the former is a million times more democratic than the most advanced capitalist democracies of the west."

Most of us want to keep our Republic. Those who desire "democracy" should go to the Soviet Union where it's a "million times more democratic . . ."

Meanwhile it might be well to stop immigration entirely. We've got a lot of digesting to do—and a bad case of indigestion.

XV.

The Anti-Defamation League of B'Nai B'Rith has been so successful in penetrating Gentile institutions of learning that it finds time to boast about it. It has adopted the "workshop technique"—and, as a consequence, the ADL "has been placed in closer cooperation than ever before with school systems, colleges and universities."

What are workshops?

Let Dr. Goslin tell us:

"I don't know that it (the workshop) ought to be designated as a substitute (for teacher's summer courses) . . . (the workshops were) set up for a period of five weeks, during which time they spend some six or seven hours a day in study consultation, in discussion groups about their problems and our problems of education . . . Teachers come to this workshop with problems . . . the workshop is a chance to put together in the local community some of the best of our own leadership results, plus some we invite from the outside, where teachers sit down with such leadership for several hours a day and work on the job of becoming better teachers." (Page 30, Eighth Report, California Senate Investigating Committee on Education.)

Outside lecturers are brought in to the workshop. The California Senate Committee on Education states (page 31, Eighth Report) that Dr. Goslin estimated the cost of the summer workshop at about $8,000 per summer. Attending teachers were paid $100 and were required to pay $60 for the course.

One of the lecturers brought to the Pasadena summer workshop was Dr. William Heard Kilpatrick, chairman of the Board of Directors of the Bureau of Intercultural Education. Says the California Senate Committee on Education (page 19): "Dr. Kilpatrick has held membership in at least seven organizations which have been listed by various Un-American Activities Committees."

And the Anti-Defamation League declares (Frank N. Trager) that "the workshop technique has been used on every teacher-training campus in the country where summer courses are given. Increasingly, it has been applied to the field of intercultural education."

It appears that Leo Shapiro, ADL's director of education, has guided the overall plan for workshop activities. Two workshops were held in Denver, jointly sponsored by the ADL and the University of Denver. "ADL men," boasts the ADL, "were regular members of the teaching staff"—thus (although the ADL is modestly silent on this point) insuring ADL indoctrination. Similar arrangements were successfully negotiated at the University of California, Rutgers, NYU, UCLA and Texas University. ADL "consultants," "such as Dr. R. B. Haas on the West Coast and Dr. Louis E. Raths in the East helped execute these plans."

From California to Florida to New England the busy little bees of the ADL traveled, "sometimes barnstorming the country" in behalf of "workshops." ADL regional directors and staff members attended more than 35 workshops and discussed problems in "intercultural" education with more than 2,000 teachers.

The cleverest part of the ADL workshop technique is that the Gentile taxpayer is compelled to pick up the check—and it cost about $8,000 a summer in Pasadena!

XVI.

Theodor Herzl, founder of modern political Zionism, declared in the bible of Zionism, *Der Judenstaat* (The Jewish State) that "the unfortunate Jews are now (1896) carrying the seeds of anti-Semitism into England; they have already introduced it into America." He was establishing the foundation upon which his movement was to rise or fall; the thesis that the Jews themselves are the cause of anti-Semitism; that they carry the seeds with them wherever they go. By way of preface Herzl asserted that "We (Jews) naturally move to those places where we are not persecuted, and there our presence produces persecution."

Chaim Weizmann, the first President of *Der Judenstaat* Israel once elaborated on Herzl's thesis. "I believe the one fundamental cause of anti-Semitism—it may seem tautological —is that the Jew exists. We seem to carry anti-Semitism in our knapsacks wherever we go. The growth and intensity of anti-Semitism is proportional to the number of Jews, or to the density of the Jews in a given country."

It must be assumed that Herzl or Weizmann were confessing Jewish vices as the cause of anti-Semitism. On the contrary they were presenting their case on the basis of *Jewish virtues;* virtues not possessed nor matched by the envious and jealous Gentiles. Persecution complexes always operate this way.

The Anti-Defamation League of B'Nai B'Rith goes much further than either Herzl or Weizmann. Using its own thinking as the norm the ADL leadership comes up with the conclusion that the overwhelming majority of Americans—three out of four or seventy-five percent of the adult population of the United States—is either actively or potentially anti-Semitic —and therefore, believe it or not,—mentally ill! Playing upon this theme—that three-quarters of the adult population of the United States is either actually insane or potentially so, the ADL and its stooges mobilize every means of propaganda to give the fantasy reality. Says Harry Allen Overstreet in an article in the *Saturday Review of Literature* republished and distributed by the Community Relations Service of New York and the Los Angeles County Committee on Human Relations: "They are intellectually and morally sick people. What is worse, they are sick people who try to make their own sickness the measure of their society's health."

It would appear, therefore, that everyone is crazy except the great Overstreet and the ADL. Hence "brain-washing" in the United States; hence the ADL dominated fronts in Mental Hygiene, Mental Health, Human and Community Relations!

Samuel Roth, himself a Jew, once wrote in substance that anti-Semitism was caused by Jewish leadership and the casual student of the problem is prone to agree with him. It is apparently the design of the scheming men who sit in places of power—in the Councils of the Anti-Defamation League of B'Nai B'Rith, the American Jewish Committee, the American Jewish Congress and the other vehicles of organized Jewry who generate the fires of discord and disruption;—that Jewry in the United States shall not be American.

The fault is not in Gentile America. "Despite our faults," declared Samuel Roth, "we would never have done so much damage to the world if it had not been for our genius for evil leadership."

XVII.

Our study of the "mental health" and "human relations" organizations—the Southern California Society for Mental Hygiene, the San Francisco Mental Health Society, the Los Angeles County Conference on Community Relations, and the Los Angeles County Committee on Human Relations, leads us to some inevitable conclusions:

Organized Jewry appears to be the moving, directing and dominating force behind each of the organizational drives for "mental health" and "human relations."

The organizations under scrutiny appear to be fronts for Jewish organizations in the same manner and probably to the same extent as the Institute for American Democracy and the Institute for Democratic Education were for the Anti-Defamation League of B'Nai B'Rith. (See *The Tenney Committee: The American Record* and *Zion's Fifth Column.*)

The personnel of all four organizations reveals the common denominator of organized Jewry—interlocking directorship and coordination.

The intent, purpose and technique approximates the dialectic Communist line long established for racial agitation. The political background of many of the leading figures in these groups give the overall movement a decided red glow unmistakable to those trained in the use of the political spectroscope. While the records cited are not offered as proof of Communist affiliation or sympathy, they do establish beyond peradventure the political bias and mental leanings of the subjects involved. Many are undoubtedly mere dupes and innocents; bleeding hearts whose brains have been washed and conditioned in the totalitarian cauldrons of New Dealism;—well intentioned individuals who find a vicarious satisfaction for deep-seated hatreds promoted under the banner of "brotherhood." This paradoxical drive is nowhere better revealed than in the words of Rabbi Leon Spitz (*The American Hebrew*, March 1, 1946): "American Jews," writes the Rabbi, "must come to grips with our contemporary anti-Semites. We must fill our jails with anti-Semitic gangsters, we must fill our insane asylums with anti-Semitic lunatics, we must combat every alien **Jew-hater,** we must harrass and persecute our Jew-baiters to the extreme limits of the laws, we must humble and shame our anti-Semitic hoodlums to such an extent that none will wish to dare to become 'fellow-travelers'." Certainly a warm expression of brotherly love designed to elicit a strong feeling of friendship in the heart of every Gentile! Rabbi Spitz's glowing tribute to "brotherhood" is in sinister contrast to the teachings of the Founder of Christianity—and the contrast is notably part of the difference. Said Jesus of Nazareth: "Ye have heard that it hath been said, Thou shalt love thy neighbor, and hate thine enemy. But I say unto you, Love your enemies, bless them that curse you, do good to them that hate you, and pray for them which despitefully use you, and persecute you."

There are many other conclusions, too numerous to summarize here, all of which are obvious to the casual reader. One, however, is of great importance and should be mentioned for emphasis. The movement indicated by the four organizations under discussion is financed from public funds;—either from Community Chest funds generously contributed by the people for other and worthy charitable purposes or from funds paid by the tax-payers for legitimate governmental functions.

Lastly it should be noted that Rabbi Spitz is crystal clear on his part—and there is nothing on record to indicate that he does not speak for organized Jewry—that Jewry must "fill our insane asylums with anti-Semitic lunatics." When it is remembered that organized Jewry looks upon the critics of Jewry as "mentally ill"—three quarters of the adult population of the United States, actively or potentially—it becomes apparent that Jewish dominated societies for "mental health" and "mental hygiene" may be busily engaged in executing Rabbi Spitz's directive.

Under ordinary circumstances the efforts of a small, almost infinitesimal fraction of society to "brain wash" the overwhelming majority of its fellow citizens or build insane asylums for them would be incredible and fantastically funny. But these are not ordinary circumstances nor ordinary times. We are in the Age of Great Delusion—when black appears white, and white appears black—when the sane are made to appear insane and the insane act as the world's psychiatrists; where, in a world of folly it is folly to be wise;—where, in the land of the blind, clear vision is a handicap.

It can happen, but it won't—because the age of delusion passes away. Things that are not what they appear become what they are and children are capable of brushing the scales from the eyes of their elders by pointing out the nakedness of the Emperor and the fraud of his non-existing suit of miraculous cloth. Clear vision must inevitably out-wit the instincts of the blind and those who dared be wise in a time of folly will be honored for the folly of having been wise. And even organized Jewry—the evil genius of the Jews everywhere—will perhaps recognize and adopt as their own the true touchstone to friendship and brotherhood: "But I say unto you, Love your enemies, bless them that curse you, do good to them that hate you, and pray for them which despitefully use you, and persecute you."

No man can long despise the man who always offers the hand of sincere friendship—and I have never heard of anyone who hated those who prayed for him—and matched their prayers with their deeds.

SENATOR JACK B. TENNEY

www.ingramcontent.com/pod-product-compliance
Lightning Source LLC
Chambersburg PA
CBHW060808280326
41934CB00010B/2611